**PIANO/VOCAL/GUITAR**

# 150 OF THE MOST BEAUTIFUL SONGS EVER

ISBN 0-88188-307-7

**HAL•LEONARD® CORPORATION**

7777 W. BLUEMOUND RD. P.O. BOX 13819 MILWAUKEE, WI 53213

Visit Hal Leonard Online at
**www.halleonard.com**

# Contents

# ALL AT ONCE YOU LOVE HER

from PIPE DREAM

Lyrics by OSCAR HAMMERSTEIN II
Music by RICHARD RODGERS

The ro- mance that you have wait- ed for will come when it comes, _ With-

out a word of warn- ing it will start. With a

sud- den blare of trum- pets and the rat- tle of drums __ A

and then you know  You'll kiss good-night for-ev-er.  You won-der where your heart can go  Then all at once you know. know.

# ALWAYS

Words and Music by
IRVING BERLIN

# ALWAYS ON MY MIND

Words and Music by WAYNE THOMPSON,
MARK JAMES and JOHNNY CHRISTOPHER

# BALI HA'I
## from SOUTH PACIFIC

Lyrics by OSCAR HAMMERSTEIN II
Music by RICHARD RODGERS

Most peo-ple live on a lone-ly is - land

Lost in the mid-dle of a fog-gy sea.

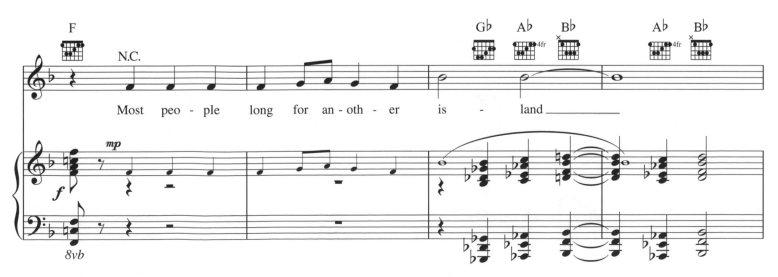

Most peo-ple long for an-oth-er is - land

# AND I LOVE HER

Words and Music by JOHN LENNON
and PAUL McCARTNEY

# AND I LOVE YOU SO

Words and Music by
DON McLEAN

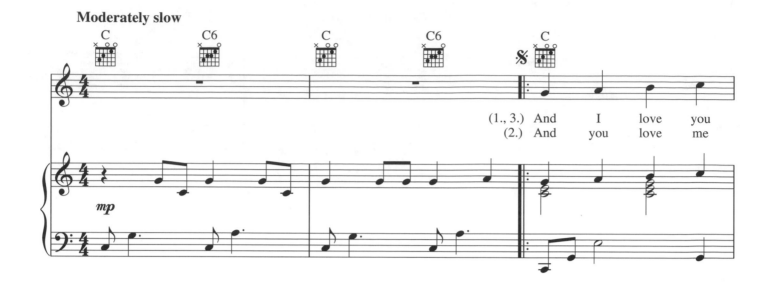

know.
do.

I guess they un-der-stand
The book of life is brief,

how lone-ly life has been,
and once a page is read,

but life be-gan a-
all but love is

gain,
dead,

the day you took my hand.
that is my be-lief.

# BEWITCHED
## from PAL JOEY

Words by LORENZ HART
Music by RICHARD RODGERS

He's a fool and don't I know it, But a fool can have his charms;

I'm in love and don't I show it, Like a babe in arms.

Love's the same old sad sen - sa - tion, Late - ly I've not slept a wink,

# BLAME IT ON MY YOUTH

Words by EDWARD HEYMAN
Music by OSCAR LEVANT

Lyrics:

You _____ were my a-dored one, then you _____ be-came the bored one, and I _____ was like a toy that brought you joy one day, _____ a bro-ken

# BODY AND SOUL

Words by EDWARD HEYMAN,
ROBERT SOUR and FRANK EYTON
Music by JOHN GREEN

# CAN'T HELP LOVIN' DAT MAN

## from SHOW BOAT

Lyrics by OSCAR HAMMERSTEIN II
Music by JEROME KERN

# BY THE TIME I GET TO PHOENIX

Words and Music by
JIMMY WEBB

# CALL ME IRRESPONSIBLE
from the Paramount Picture PAPA'S DELICATE CONDITION

Words by SAMMY CAHN
Music by JAMES VAN HEUSEN

# CANDLE IN THE WIND

Music by ELTON JOHN
Words by BERNIE TAUPIN

**Gently, reflectively**

Good-bye Nor - ma Jean, _____ though I nev - er
Lone - li - ness _____ was tough, _____ the tough - est role

knew you _____ at all you had the grace to hold your-self _____ while
you ev - er played. Hol - ly-wood cre - at - ed a su - per-star _____ and

those a - round _____ you crawled. _____ They crawled out of the
pain was the price you paid. _____ E - ven when you

# CLIMB EV'RY MOUNTAIN
## from THE SOUND OF MUSIC

Lyrics by OSCAR HAMMERSTEIN II
Music by RICHARD RODGERS

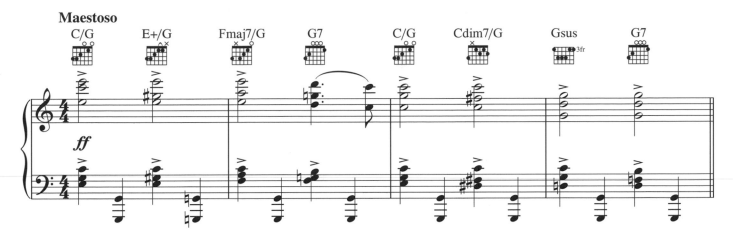

# (They Long to Be)
# CLOSE TO YOU

Lyric by HAL DAVID
Music by BURT BACHARACH

# DADDY'S LITTLE GIRL

Words and Music by BOBBY BURKE
and HORACE GERLACH

Lit - tle girl of mine, with eyes of shin-ing blue, Lit - tle girl of

mine, I love you, yes, I do; No one else could

be so sweet, You have made my life com -

# A DREAM IS A WISH YOUR HEART MAKES

from Walt Disney's CINDERELLA

Words and Music by MACK DAVID,
AL HOFFMAN and JERRY LIVINGSTON

When I was a lit- tle {girl, boy,} my fa- ther used to

say, if trou- ble ev- er trou- bles you, just dream your cares a-

way. A dream is a wish your heart makes ____

# ENDLESS LOVE
## from ENDLESS LOVE

Words and Music by
LIONEL RICHIE

# FEELINGS
## (¿Dime?)

English Words and Music by MORRIS ALBERT
and LOUIS GASTE
Spanish Words by THOMAS FUNDORA

**Moderately Slow**

Feel - ings, \_\_\_
Tear - drops \_\_\_

noth - ing more than Feel - ings, \_\_\_
roll - ing down on my face, \_\_\_

try - ing to for - get my
try - ing to for - get _____ my

feel-ings of
feel-ings of

love.

love.

# FIELDS OF GOLD

Music and Lyrics by
STING

**Flowing, moderately**

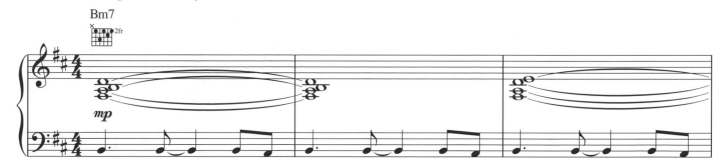

You'll re-mem-ber me, when the west wind moves _ up-a-
stay with me, will you be my love _ a-

on the fields _ of bar-ley. You'll for-get the sun in his
mong the fields _ of bar-ley? We'll for-get the sun in his

Man - y years have passed since those ___
mem - ber me when the ___

___ sum - mer days a - mong the fields ___ of bar - ley. See the
___ west wind moves up - on the fields ___ of bar - ley. You can

# THE FIRST TIME EVER I SAW YOUR FACE

Words and Music by
EWAN MacCOLL

# THE FOLKS WHO LIVE ON THE HILL

## from HIGH, WIDE AND HANDSOME

Lyrics by OSCAR HAMMERSTEIN II
Music by JEROME KERN

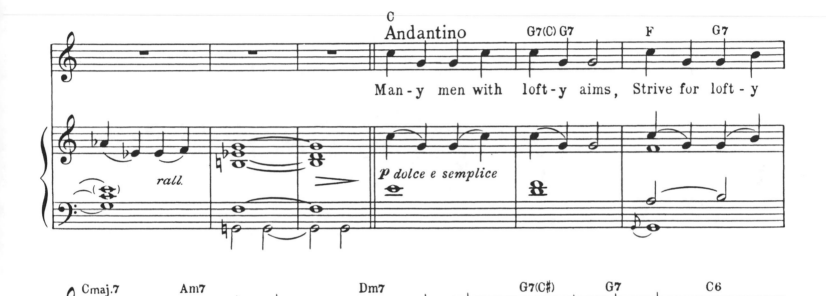

Man-y men with loft-y aims, Strive for loft-y

goals, Oth-ers play at small-er games, Be-ing simp-ler souls.

I am of the lat-ter brand; All I want to do Is to find a spot of land

# FLY ME TO THE MOON
## (In Other Words)
### featured in the Motion Picture ONCE AROUND

Words and Music by
BART HOWARD

# FROM A DISTANCE

Words and Music by
JULIE GOLD

# GOOD MORNING HEARTACHE

Words and Music by DAN FISHER,
IRENE HIGGINBOTHAM and ERVIN DRAKE

Good morn-ing heart-ache, you old gloom-y sight. Good morn-ing heart-ache, tho't we said good-bye last night. I tossed and turned un-til it seemed you had gone, but here you are with the dawn. Wish I'd for-get you

# GEORGIA ON MY MIND

Words by STUART GORRELL
Music by HOAGY CARMICHAEL

# GOD ONLY KNOWS

Words and Music by BRIAN WILSON
and TONY ASHER

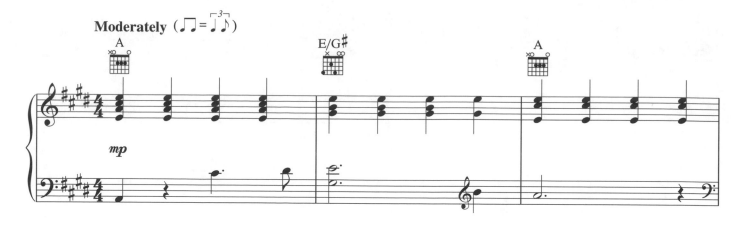

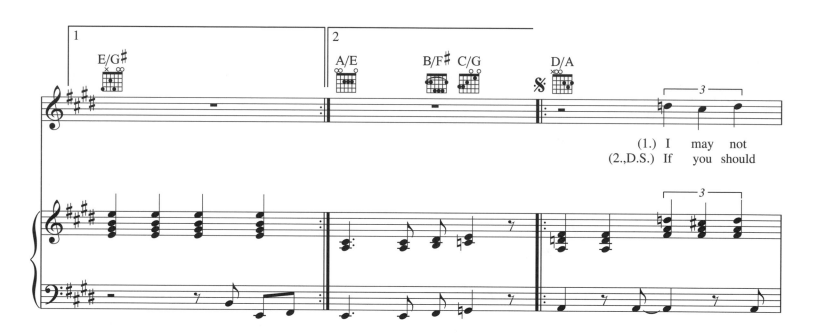

(1.) I may not
(2.,D.S.) If you should

al - ways love _ you,          but long as there are _ stars    a - bove you,
ev - er leave _ me,          well, life would still go _ on,  be - lieve me.

# GOOD NIGHT

Words and Music by JOHN LENNON
and PAUL McCARTNEY

# HERE'S THAT RAINY DAY
## from CARNIVAL IN FLANDERS

Words by JOHNNY BURKE
Music by JIMMY VAN HEUSEN

# HOW ARE THINGS IN GLOCCA MORRA

## from FINIAN'S RAINBOW

Words by E.Y. HARBURG
Music by BURTON LANE

# HOW DEEP IS THE OCEAN

## (How High Is the Sky)

Words and Music by
IRVING BERLIN

Lyrics:
How much do I love you? I'll tell you no lie, how deep is the o - cean, how high is the sky? How man - y

# HOW DEEP IS YOUR LOVE

from the Motion Picture SATURDAY NIGHT FEVER

Words and Music by ROBIN GIBB,
MAURICE GIBB and BARRY GIBB

I know your eyes in the morn-ing sun.___ I feel you touch___
I be-lieve in you.___ You know the door___

___ me in the pour-ing rain.___ And the mo-ment that you wan-der far___
___ to my ver-y soul.___ You're the light___ in my deep-est, dark-

___ from me,___ I wan-na feel you in my arms a-gain. And you come___
-est hour;___ you're my sav-ior when I fall.___ And you may___

# I CAN'T GET STARTED WITH YOU

## from ZIEGFELD FOLLIES

Words by IRA GERSHWIN
Music by VERNON DUKE

Lyrics:
I'm a glum one, it's explainable: I met someone unattainable. Life's a bore, the world is my oyster no

# I HAVE DREAMED

## from THE KING AND I

Lyrics by OSCAR HAMMERSTEIN II
Music by RICHARD RODGERS

# I HONESTLY LOVE YOU

Words and Music by PETER ALLEN
and JEFF BARRY

May-be I hang a-round ___ here a lit-tle more than I should; we
You don't ___ have to an - swer; I see it in your eyes.

both know I got some - where else ___ to go. But
May - be it was bet - ter left ___ un - said. But

# I JUST CALLED TO SAY I LOVE YOU

Words and Music by
STEVIE WONDER

1. No New Year's Day          to cel - e -
3.,4. (See additional lyrics)

brate;          no flow - ers
rain;

no choc - 'late cov - ered can - dy hearts
no wed - ding Sat - ur - day ___ with - in ___

to give ___ a - way. ___          No first of
the month ___ of June. ___          But what it

140

*Additional Lyrics*

3. No summer's high; no warm July;
   No harvest moon to light one tender August night.
   No autumn breeze; no falling leaves;
   Not even time for birds to fly to southern skies.

4. No Libra sun; no Halloween;
   No giving thanks to all the Christmas joy you bring.
   But what it is, though old so new
   To fill your heart like no three words could ever do.
   *Chorus*

# I LEFT MY HEART IN SAN FRANCISCO

Words by DOUGLASS CROSS
Music by GEORGE CORY

# I WON'T LAST A DAY WITHOUT YOU

Words and Music by PAUL WILLIAMS
and ROGER NICHOLS

Moderately slow

Day af-ter day ___ I must face a world ___ of strang-ers where I
So man-y times ___ when the cit-y seems ___ to be with-out a

don't be-long; ___ I'm not that strong. It's nice to know ___ that there's
friend-ly face, ___ a lone-ly place, it's nice to know ___ that you'll

some-one I ___ can turn to who will al-ways care; ___ you're
be there if ___ I need you, and you'll al-ways smile; ___ it's

*Vocal sung one octave lower than written.

# I WANT YOU, I NEED YOU, I LOVE YOU

Words by MAURICE MYSELS
Music by IRA KOSLOFF

Moderately Slow

# I WILL WAIT FOR YOU

## from THE UMBRELLAS OF CHERBOURG

Music by MICHEL LEGRAND
Original French Text by JACQUES DEMY
English Words by NORMAN GIMBEL

# I WISH YOU LOVE

English Words by ALBERT BEACH
French Words and Music by CHARLES TRENET

# I'LL BE SEEING YOU

## from RIGHT THIS WAY

Lyric by IRVING KAHAL
Music by SAMMY FAIN

Ca-the-dral bells were toll-ing _____ And our hearts sang on, _____

Was it the spell of Par-is _____ Or the A-pril dawn? _____

Who knows, _____ if we shall meet a-gain?

# I'LL HAVE TO SAY I LOVE YOU IN A SONG

Words and Music by
JIM CROCE

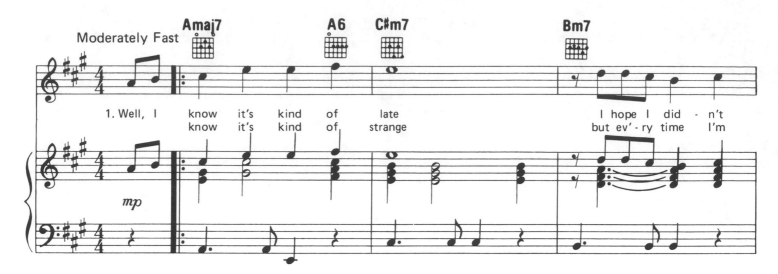

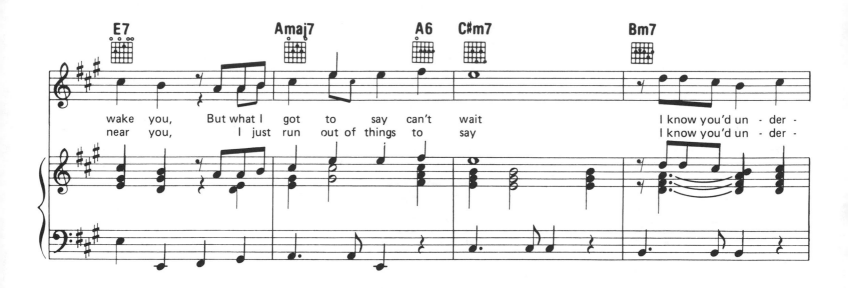

# I'LL NEVER SMILE AGAIN

Words and Music by
RUTH LOWE

You loved me in the past, but our ro-mance did-n't last. You thrilled me with your kiss, dar-ling, now _____ I prom-ise this: I'll nev-er smile a-gain un-til I smile at you. _____

# I'LL REMEMBER APRIL

Words and Music by PAT JOHNSON,
DON RAYE and GENE DE PAUL

# I'VE GOT YOU UNDER MY SKIN

## from BORN TO DANCE

Words and Music by
COLE PORTER

# IMAGINATION

Words by JOHNNY BURKE
Music by JIMMY VAN HEUSEN

# I'VE GROWN ACCUSTOMED TO HER FACE

### from MY FAIR LADY

Words by ALAN JAY LERNER
Music by FREDERICK LOEWE

# IF YOU GO AWAY

French Words and Music by JACQUES BREL
English Words by ROD McKUEN

# IN MY ROOM

Words and Music by BRIAN WILSON
and GARY USHER

**Moderately slow**

There's a world where I can go and
In this world where I lock out all my
Now it's dark and I'm a - lone but

tell my se - crets to,
wor - ries and my fears
I won't be a - fraid,

in my room,

in my

# IN THE WEE SMALL HOURS OF THE MORNING

Words by BOB HILLIARD
Music by DAVID MANN

**Slowly, with restraint**

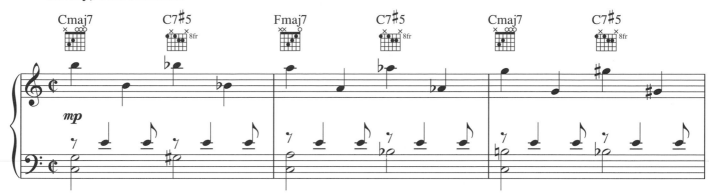

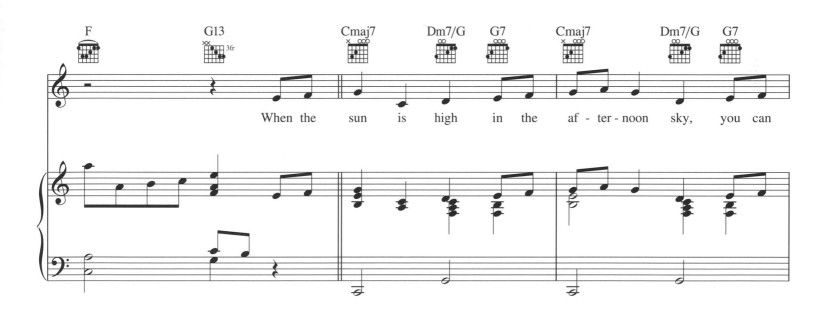

When the sun is high in the af-ter-noon sky, you can

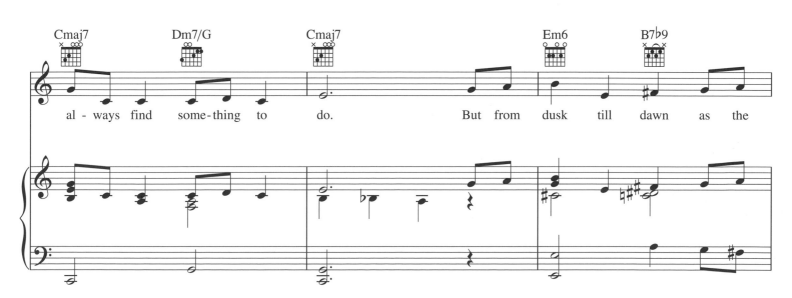

al-ways find some-thing to do. But from dusk till dawn as the

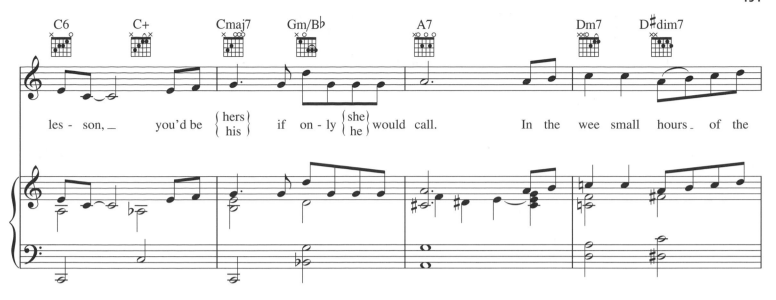

les - son, __ you'd be {hers}{his} if on - ly {she}{he} would call. In the wee small hours __ of the

morn - ing __ that's the way you miss {her}{him} most of all. In the

time you miss {her}{him} most of all. __

# IN THE STILL OF THE NIGHT

from ROSALIE
from NIGHT AND DAY

Words and Music by
COLE PORTER

# ISN'T IT ROMANTIC?

from the Paramount Picture LOVE ME TONIGHT

Words by LORENZ HART
Music by RICHARD RODGERS

# IT MIGHT AS WELL BE SPRING

## from STATE FAIR

Lyrics by OSCAR HAMMERSTEIN II
Music by RICHARD RODGERS

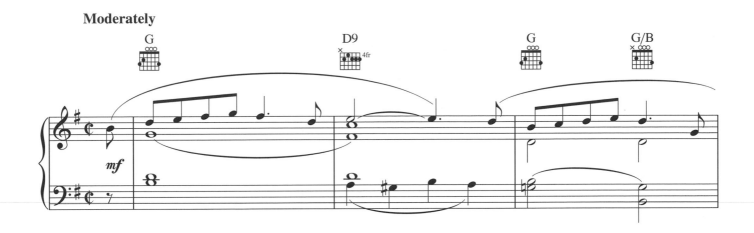

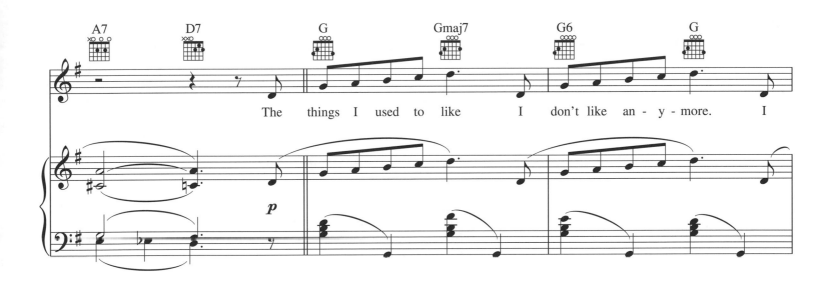

The things I used to like I don't like an-y-more. I

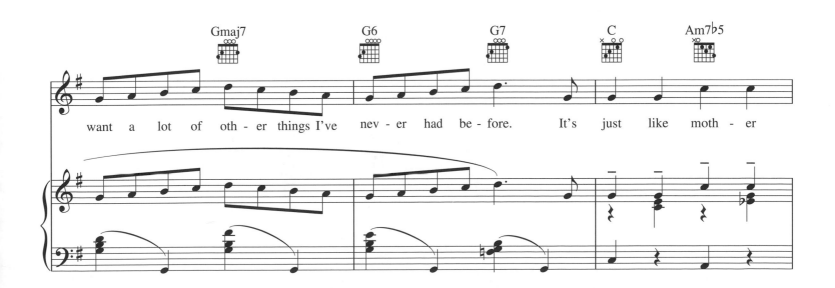

want a lot of oth-er things I've nev-er had be-fore. It's just like moth-er

# IT'S A BLUE WORLD

Words and Music by BOB WRIGHT
and CHET FORREST

# THE LAST TIME I SAW PARIS

from LADY, BE GOOD
from TILL THE CLOUDS ROLL BY

Lyrics by OSCAR HAMMERSTEIN II
Music by JEROME KERN

# THE LAST WALTZ

Words and Music by LES REED
and BARRY MASON

# LET IT BE ME
## (Je T'appartiens)

English Words by MANN CURTIS
French Words by PIERRE DeLANOE
Music by GILBERT BECAUD

Relaxed

I bless the day I found you, I want to stay a-round you,
If, for each day bit of glad - ness, Some - one must taste of sad - ness,

And so I beg you, let it be me. Don't take this
I'll bear the sor - row, let it be me. No mat - ter

heav - en from one, If you must cling to some - one, Now and for - ev - er,
what the price is, I'll make the sac - ri - fic - es, Through each to - mor - row,

# LILLI MARLENE

German Lyric by HANS LEIP
English Lyric by TOMMIE CONNOR
Music by NORBERT SCHULTZE

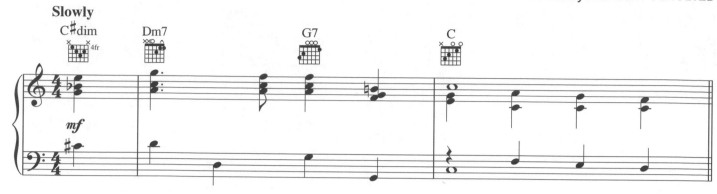

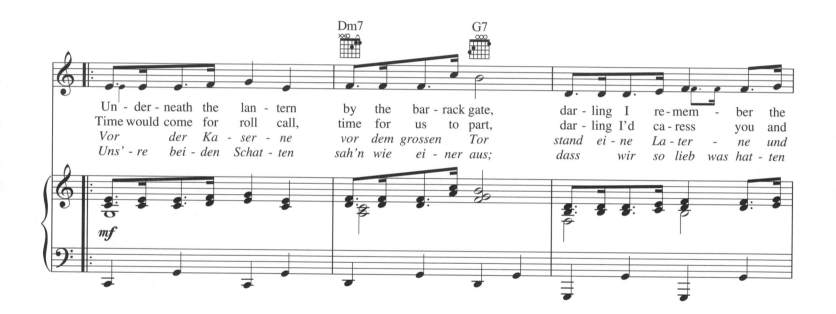

Un - der - neath the lan - tern by the bar - rack gate,
Time would come for roll call, time for us to part,
*Vor der Ka - ser - ne vor dem grossen Tor*
*Uns' - re bei - den Schat - ten sah'n wie ei - ner aus;*

dar - ling I re - mem - ber the
dar - ling I'd ca - ress you and
*stand ei - ne La - ter - ne und*
*dass wir so lieb was hat - ten*

way you used to wait. 'Twas there that you whis - pered ten - der - ly that
press you to my heart. And there 'neath that far off lan - tern light I'd
*steht sie noch da - ror, So woll'n wir da uns wie - der - sehn, bei*
*sah man gleich da - raus. Und al - le Leu - te soll'n es sehn wenn*

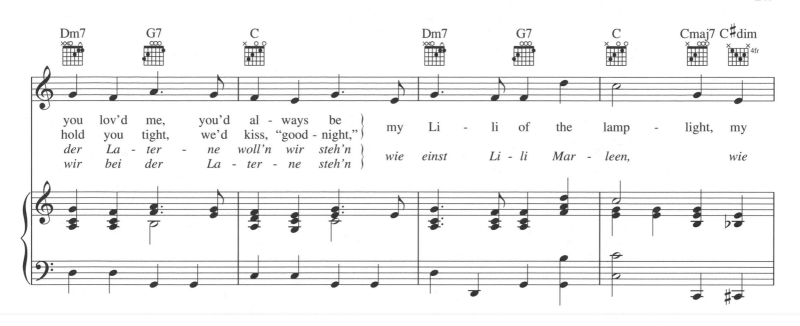

you lov'd me, you'd al - ways be ) my Li - li of the lamp - light, my
hold you tight, we'd kiss, "good - night," )
*der La - ter - ne woll'n wir steh'n )* *wie einst Li - li Mar - leen,* *wie*
*wir bei der La - ter - ne steh'n )*

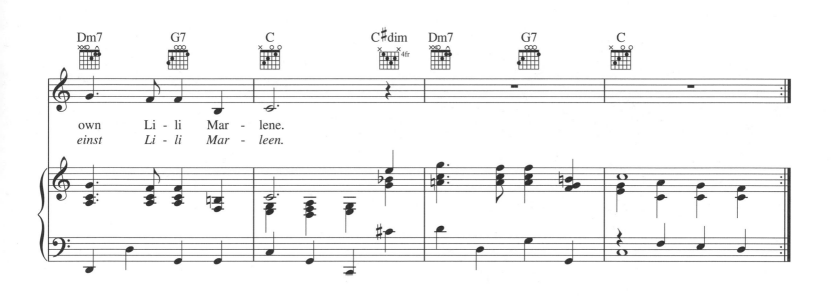

own Li - li Mar - lene.
*einst Li - li Mar - leen.*

Or - ders came for sail - ing some - where o - ver there, all con - fined to bar - racks was
Rest - ing in a bill - et just be - hind the line, e - ven tho' we're part - ed your
*Schon rief der Po - sten: sie bla - sen Za - pfen sheich; es kann drei Ta - ge ko - sten! Ka - me*
*Dei - ne Schrit - te kennt sie, dei - nen zie - ren Gang, al - le A - bend brennt sie*
*Aus dem stil - lin Rau - me, aus der Er - de Grund hebt mich wie im Trau - me*

# LOLLIPOPS AND ROSES

Words and Music by
TONY VELONA

# LITTLE GIRL BLUE

**from JUMBO**

Words by LORENZ HART
Music by RICHARD RODGERS

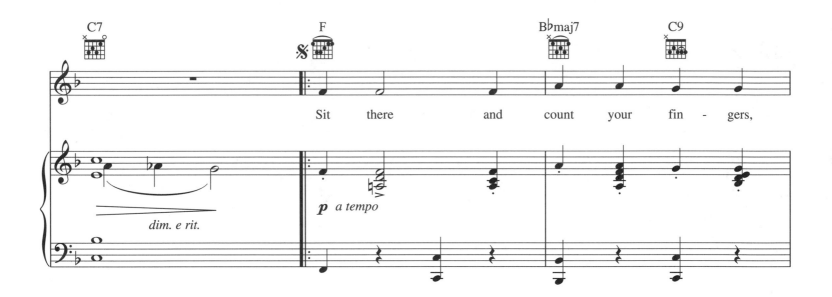

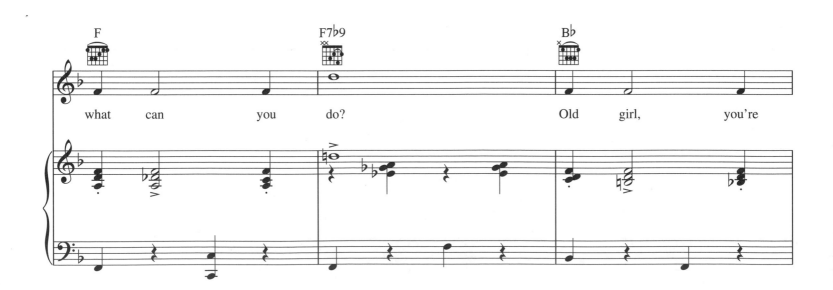

young - er than I, As mer - ry as a car - ou - sel. The cir - cus tent was strung with ev - 'ry star in the sky A - bove the ring

# LONGER

Words and Music by
DAN FOGELBERG

Long-er than __ there've been fish-es in the o-cean,
Strong-er than __ an-y moun-tain ca-the-dral,
Through the years __ as the fi-re starts to mel-low,

high-er than __ an-y bird ev-er flew, __
tru-er than __ an-y tree ev-er grew, __
burn-ing lines __ in the book of our lives. __

Long-er than __ there've been
Deep-er than __ an-y
Though the bind-ing cracks __ and the pag-

# LOOK TO THE RAINBOW

## from FINIAN'S RAINBOW

Words by E.Y. HARBURG
Music by BURTON LANE

234

# LOVE, LOOK AWAY

## from FLOWER DRUM SONG

Lyrics by OSCAR HAMMERSTEIN II
Music by RICHARD RODGERS

# LOVING YOU

Words and Music by JERRY LEIBER
and MIKE STOLLER

*Even eighth notes.

# LULLABY OF THE LEAVES

Words by JOE YOUNG
Music by BERNICE PETKERE

# MANHATTAN
from the Broadway Musical THE GARRICK GAIETIES

Words by LORENZ HART
Music by RICHARD RODGERS

# MEMORY
## from CATS

Music by ANDREW LLOYD WEBBER
Text by TREVOR NUNN after T.S. ELIOT

**GRIZABELLA:**

Mid - night. _____ Not a sound from the pave - ment. _____ Has the moon lost her

Mem - ory _____ all a - lone in the moon - light _____ I can smile at the

mem - ory? _____ She is smil-ing a - lone. _____ In the

old days, _____ I was beau-ti-ful then. _____ I re -

Burnt out ends of smo - ky days, ___ the stale cold smell ___ of

sun. _____ If you touch me you'll un-der-stand what

hap-pi-ness is. Look a new day has be-

gun.

# MEMORIES OF YOU
## from THE BENNY GOODMAN STORY

Lyric by ANDY RAZAF
Music by EUBIE BLAKE

Moderately slow

# MIDNIGHT BLUE

Words and Music by CAROL BAYER SAGER
and MELISSA MANCHESTER

Whatever it is, it'll keep till the morning.
all of the times you told me you need me,

Haven't we both got better things to do?
needing me now is something I could use.

Midnight blue.
Midnight blue.

Even though simple things become rough,
Wouldn't you give your hand to a friend?

# MONA LISA

from the Paramount Picture CAPTAIN CAREY, U.S.A.

Words and Music by JAY LIVINGSTON
and RAY EVANS

In a vil - la in a lit - tle old I - tal - ian town

lives a girl whose beau - ty shames the rose.

Man - y yearn to love her but their

hopes all tum - ble down

What does she want? No one knows!

Mo - na

# MOON RIVER

## from the Paramount Picture BREAKFAST AT TIFFANY'S

Words by JOHNNY MERCER
Music by HENRY MANCINI

# MOONLIGHT IN VERMONT

Words and Music by JOHN BLACKBURN
and KARL SUESSDORF

# MORE
## (Ti Guarderò Nel Cuore)
### from the film MONDO CANE

Music by NINO OLIVIERO and RIZ ORTOLANI
Italian Lyrics by MARCELLO CIORCIOLINI
English Lyrics by NORMAN NEWELL

# MY CHERIE AMOUR

Words and Music by STEVIE WONDER,
SYLVIA MOY and HENRY COSBY

dis - tant as the Milk - y Way. _____ My Che -
nev - er no - ticed me. _____ My Che -
share your lit - tle dis - tant cloud. _____ Oh, Che -

rie A - mour, _ pret - ty lit - tle one that I _____ a - dore, _
rie A - mour, _ won't you tell me how could you _____ ig - nore _
rie A - mour, _ pret - ty lit - tle one that I _____ a - dore, _

you're the on - ly girl my heart _____ beats for; _____ how I wish that you were mine. _
that be - hind that lit - tle smile _____ I wore, _ how I wish that you were mine. _
you're the on - ly girl my heart _____ beats for; _____ how I wish that you were mine. _

# MY FUNNY VALENTINE
## from BABES IN ARMS

Words by LORENZ HART
Music by RICHARD RODGERS

# MY ONE AND ONLY LOVE

Words by ROBERT MELLIN
Music by GUY WOOD

# MY ROMANCE
## from JUMBO

Words by LORENZ HART
Music by RICHARD RODGERS

# THE NEARNESS OF YOU

### from the Paramount Picture ROMANCE IN THE DARK

Words by NED WASHINGTON
Music by HOAGY CARMICHAEL

Gm7  C7  Fmaj7  Cm7  Cm7/F  F7#5

It is-n't your sweet con-ver-sa-tion that

Bbmaj7  Bbdim7  Bbm  Am7  Ab7

brings this sen-sa-tion. Oh, no _____

Gm7  C7  F6

___ it's just the near-ness of you. _____

Gm7b5

___ When you're in my arms _____

# OH, WHAT A BEAUTIFUL MORNIN'

## from OKLAHOMA!

Lyrics by OSCAR HAMMERSTEIN II
Music by RICHARD RODGERS

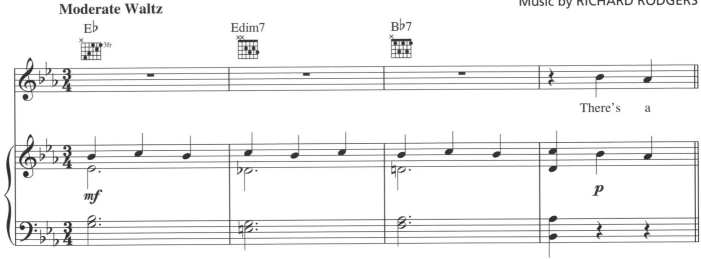

**Moderate Waltz**

There's a

bright gold - en haze on the mead - ow, _____
cat - tle are stand - in' like stat - ues, _____
sounds of the earth are like mu - sic, _____

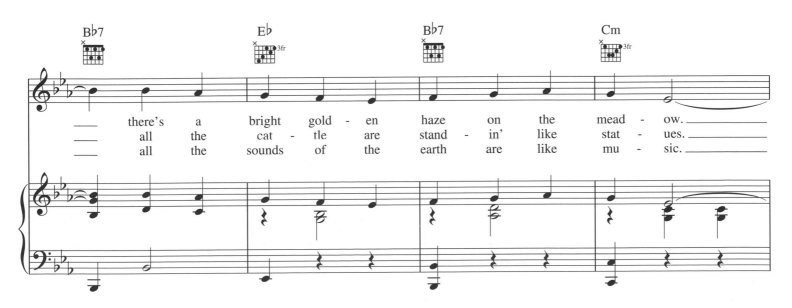

_____ there's a bright gold - en haze on the mead - ow.
_____ all the cat - tle are stand - in' like stat - ues.
_____ all the sounds of the earth are like mu - sic.

# OLD DEVIL MOON
## from FINIAN'S RAINBOW

Words by E.Y. HARBURG
Music by BURTON LANE

# THE PARTY'S OVER
## from BELLS ARE RINGING

Words by BETTY COMDEN and ADOLPH GREEN
Music by JULE STYNE

Moderately

The par-ty's o- ver, It's time to call it a day. They've burst your pret-ty bal-loon and tak-en the moon a- way. It's time to wind up the mas-quer-ade. Just make your mind up The pip-er

# PEOPLE
## from FUNNY GIRL

Words by BOB MERRILL
Music by JULE STYNE

# PEOPLE WILL SAY WE'RE IN LOVE

## from OKLAHOMA!

Lyrics by OSCAR HAMMERSTEIN II
Music by RICHARD RODGERS

**Em** **A7** **Dm** **D7**

prove what they say is quite un - true.
carved our i - ni - tials on the tree!

**G** **Gm** **D** **D/C**

Here is the gist, a prac - ti - cal list of "don'ts" for
Jist keep a slice of all the ad - vice you give so

**G/B** **G7** **C**

you. Don't throw _____ bou - quets at me.
free. Don't praise _____ my charm too much.

**G7**

Don't please _____ my folks too much.
Don't look _____ so vain with me.

*mf*

# POLKA DOTS AND MOONBEAMS

Words by JOHNNY BURKE
Music by JIMMY VAN HEUSEN

# PUT YOUR HEAD ON MY SHOULDER

Words and Music by
PAUL ANKA

Put your head on my should-er,
Hold me in your arms, Ba-by.

Squeeze me oh so tight,
Show me that you love me too.

Put your lips close to mine, dear.
Won't you kiss me once, Ba-by?

# THE RAINBOW CONNECTION
## from THE MUPPET MOVIE

Words and Music by PAUL WILLIAMS
and KENNETH L. ASCHER

# RAINY DAYS AND MONDAYS

Lyrics by PAUL WILLIAMS
Music by ROGER NICHOLS

**D.S. al Coda**

Rain - y days and Mon - days al - ways get me ___ down. _____

**CODA**

What I feel has come ___ and gone ___ be -

fore. No need to talk it out. ___

We know what it's all a - bout. ___ Hang - in' a - round, ___

Lyrics:

noth-in' to do but frown. Rain-y days and Mon-days al - ways get me down.

Hang-in' a - round, noth-in' to do but frown.

Rain-y days and Mon-days al - ways get me down.

# RETURN TO ME

Words and Music by DANNY DI MINNO
and CARMEN LOMBARDO

# RELEASE ME

Words and Music by ROBERT YOUNT,
EDDIE MILLER and DUB WILLIAMS

# SEPTEMBER SONG
from the Musical Play KNICKERBOCKER HOLIDAY

Words by MAXWELL ANDERSON
Music by KURT WEILL

Oh it's a long, long while From May to De- cem- ber,___

But the days grow short,_____ When you reach Sep- tem- ber,___

When the au- tumn wea- ther___ turns the leaves to flame,

# SHE

Lyric by HERBERT KRETZMER
Music by CHARLES AZNAVOUR

Moderately

# SINCE I DON'T HAVE YOU

Words and Music by JAMES BEAUMONT,
JANET VOGEL, JOSEPH VERSCHAREN,
WALTER LESTER, LENNIE MARTIN,
JOSEPH ROCK and JOHN TAYLOR

# SINCERELY

Words and Music by ALAN FREED
and HARVEY FUQUA

# SKYLARK

Words by JOHNNY MERCER
Music by HOAGY CARMICHAEL

# SMOKE GETS IN YOUR EYES

from ROBERTA

Words by OTTO HARBACH
Music by JEROME KERN

# SMALL WORLD

## from GYPSY

Words by STEPHEN SONDHEIM
Music by JULE STYNE

# SMILE
## Theme from MODERN TIMES

Words by JOHN TURNER and GEOFFREY PARSONS
Music by CHARLES CHAPLIN

Moderately, with great warmth

Smile, tho' your heart is ach - ing, smile, e - ven tho' it's break - ing. When there are clouds in the sky, you'll get by, if you smile through your fear and sor - row, smile and may - be to - mor - row, you'll see the sun come shin - ing

# SO IN LOVE
## from KISS ME, KATE

Words and Music by
COLE PORTER

# SOME ENCHANTED EVENING

### from SOUTH PACIFIC

Lyrics by OSCAR HAMMERSTEIN II
Music by RICHARD RODGERS

Some en-chant-ed eve-ning ____ You may see a stran-ger, ____

You may see a stran-ger ____ A-cross a

# SOME DAY MY PRINCE WILL COME

Words by LARRY MOREY
Music by FRANK CHURCHILL

# SOMETHING WONDERFUL

## from THE KING AND I

Lyrics by OSCAR HAMMERSTEIN II
Music by RICHARD RODGERS

give and for - give and help and pro - tect, as long _____ as you

**Moderato**

live. _____

**Refrain** *(slowly, with expression)*

He will not al - ways say What you would have him say,

But, now and then, he'll say some - thing won - der - ful.

# SOMEWHERE, MY LOVE
## Lara's Theme from DOCTOR ZHIVAGO

Lyric by PAUL FRANCIS WEBSTER
Music by MAURICE JARRE

Moderately, with expression

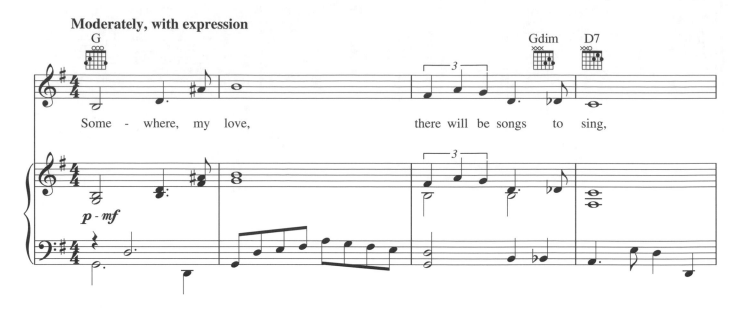

Some - where, my love, there will be songs to sing,

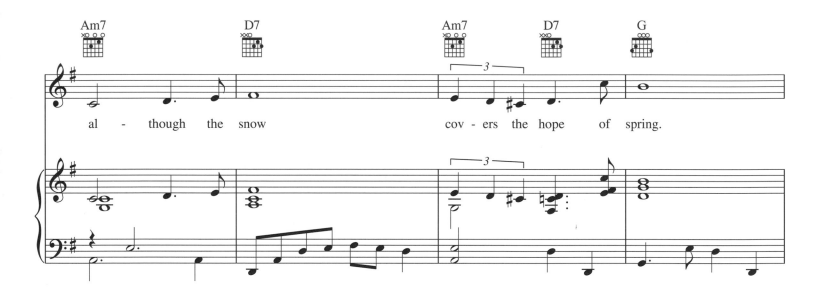

al - though the snow cov - ers the hope of spring.

Some - where a hill blos - soms in green and gold,

# SOMEWHERE OUT THERE

### from AN AMERICAN TAIL

Words and Music by JAMES HORNER,
BARRY MANN and CYNTHIA WEIL

# SPANISH EYES

Words by CHARLES SINGLETON and EDDIE SNYDER
Music by BERT KAEMPFERT

# SPEAK LOW

from the Musical Production ONE TOUCH OF VENUS

Words by OGDEN NASH
Music by KURT WEILL

# SPEAK SOFTLY, LOVE
## (Love Theme)
### from the Paramount Picture THE GODFATHER

Words by LARRY KUSIK
Music by NINO ROTA

Speak soft-ly, love, and hold me warm a-gainst your heart. I feel your words, the ten-der, trem-bling mo-ments start. We're in a world our ver-y own, shar-ing a love that on-ly few have ev-er known. Wine-col-ored

# STARDUST

Words by MITCHELL PARISH
Music by HOAGY CARMICHAEL

...And now the pur-ple dusk of twi-light time steals a-cross the mead-ows of my heart. High up in the sky the lit-tle stars climb, al-ways re-mind-ing me that

F6
Fm6
wonder why I spend the lonely night
C
Em7
A7
dreaming of a song? The melody haunts my reverie,
Dm7
A7
Dm7
Fm6
and I am once again with you, when our
G7
Gdim7
G7
G7♯5
C
love was new, and each kiss an inspiration.

# STRANGERS IN THE NIGHT
adapted from A MAN COULD GET KILLED

Words by CHARLES SINGLETON
and EDDIE SNYDER
Music by BERT KAEMPFERT

Stran-gers in the night _____ ex-chang-ing glanc-es, won-d'ring in the night _____ what were the chanc-es we'd be shar-ing love _____ be-fore the night was through. _____ Some-thing in your eyes _____ was so in-vit-ing,

love was just a glance a-way, a warm em-brac-ing dance a-way. And ev-er since that night _____

_____ we've been to-geth-er, lov-ers at first sight _____ in love for-ev-er.

It turned out so right _____ for stran-gers in the night.

night. _____

# STELLA BY STARLIGHT
## from the Paramount Picture THE UNINVITED

Words by NED WASHINGTON
Music by VICTOR YOUNG

# A SUNDAY KIND OF LOVE

Words and Music BY BARBARA BELLE, LOUIS PRIMA,
ANITA LEONARD and STAN RHODES

# TEARS IN HEAVEN

Words and Music by ERIC CLAPTON
and WILL JENNINGS

Be - yond the door _____ there's peace, I'm sure, _

# TAMMY
## from TAMMY AND THE BACHELOR

Words and Music by
JAY LIVINGSTON and RAY EVANS

# TENDERLY

from TORCH SONG

Lyric by JACK LAWRENCE
Music by WALTER GROSS

# TENNESSEE WALTZ

Words and Music by REDD STEWART
and PEE WEE KING

# THERE'S A SMALL HOTEL
## from ON YOUR TOES

Words by LORENZ HART
Music by RICHARD RODGERS

stee - ple bell says, "Good - night, sleep well," we'll

thank the small ho - tel to - geth - er. _____

tel. _____ We'll creep in - to our lit - tle shell _____ And we will

thank the small ho - tel to - geth - er. _____

# THESE FOOLISH THINGS
## (Remind Me of You)

Words by HOLT MARVELL
Music by JACK STRACHEY

# A TIME FOR US
## (Love Theme)
### from the Paramount Picture ROMEO AND JULIET

Words by LARRY KUSIK and EDDIE SNYDER
Music by NINO ROTA

# THE THINGS WE DID LAST SUMMER

Words by SAMMY CAHN
Music by JULE STYNE

# TILL THERE WAS YOU
## from Meredith Willson's THE MUSIC MAN

By MEREDITH WILLSON

Rubato · mp

Moderately Fast

Ebmaj7 · Edim · Fm7 · Abm7

There were bells on the hill, but I nev- er heard them ring- ing. No, I

Eb · Ebmaj7 · Dmaj7 · Fm7 · Bb7 · Gm7 · Gb7 · Fm7 · Bb7

nev- er heard them at all 'till there was you. _____ There were

Ebmaj7 · Edim · Fm7 · Abm7

birds in the sky, but I nev- er saw them wing- ing, No, I

# TIME IN A BOTTLE

Words and Music by
JIM CROCE

# TRUE LOVE
## from HIGH SOCIETY

Words and Music by
COLE PORTER

# TRY TO REMEMBER
## from THE FANTASTICKS

Words by TOM JONES
Music by HARVEY SCHMIDT

Slowly, with tenderness

Try to re-mem-ber the kind of Sep-tem-ber when life was
Try to re-mem-ber the kind of when life was so ten-der that no one

slow and oh, so mel-low.___ Try to re-mem-ber the
wept ex-cept the wil-low.___ Try to re-mem-ber the

kind of Sep-tem-ber when grass was green and grain was yel-low___
life was so ten-der that dreams were kept be-side your pil-low___

# THE TWELFTH OF NEVER

Words by PAUL FRANCIS WEBSTER
Music by JERRY LIVINGSTON

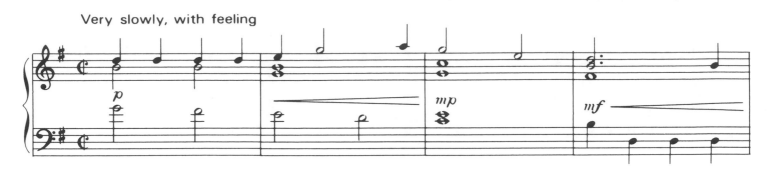

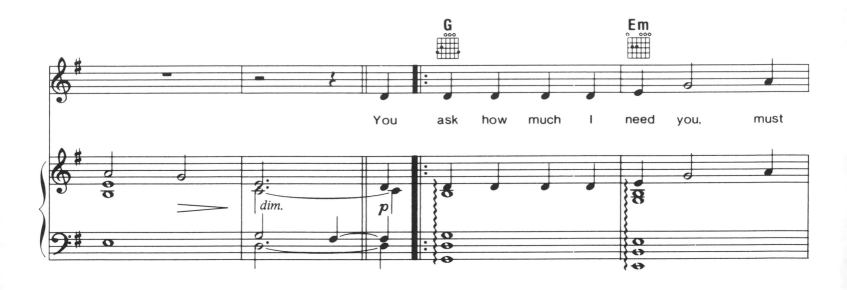

You ask how much I need you, must

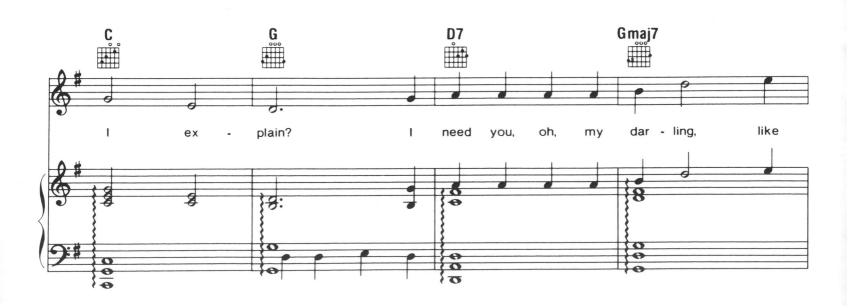

I ex - plain? I need you, oh, my dar - ling, like

# UNCHAINED MELODY
### from the Motion Picture UNCHAINED

Lyric by HY ZARET
Music by ALEX NORTH

F
G
C
I'll be com - in' home. Wait for me!"
Am
Woah, my love, my
F
G
dar - lin', I've hun - gered, hun - gered for your
C
Am
touch a long, lone - ly

# UNTIL IT'S TIME FOR YOU TO GO

Words and Music by
BUFFY SAINTE-MARIE

now. _____ This love of mine had no be - gin - ning, it has no

end, _____ I was an oak, now I'm a wil - low; now I can

bend. _____ And though I'll nev - er in my life see you a -

gain, _____ still I'll stay un-til it's time for you to go. _____ Don't ask \_\_ why of me, don't ask \_\_ how of

# THE VERY THOUGHT OF YOU

Words and Music by
RAY NOBLE

I don't need your pho-to-graph,
to keep by my bed;
al-ways in my head.

I hold you re-spon-si-ble,
I'll take it to law,
felt like this be-fore.

Your pic-ture is
I nev-er have

# The Way You Look Tonight

## from SWING TIME

Words by DOROTHY FIELDS
Music by JEROME KERN

# WE KISS IN A SHADOW

## from THE KING AND I

Lyrics by OSCAR HAMMERSTEIN II
Music by RICHARD RODGERS

**Molto moderato e semplice**

**Refrain** *(slowly and tenderly)*

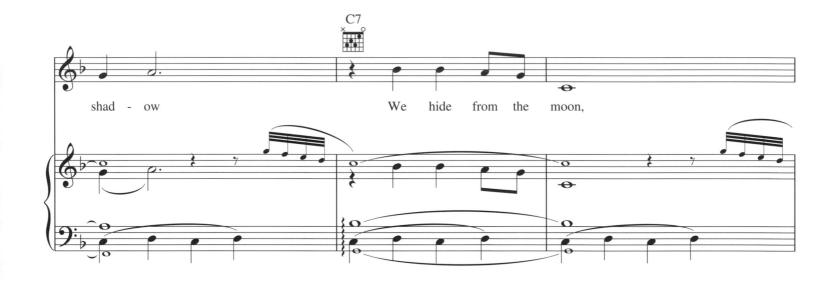

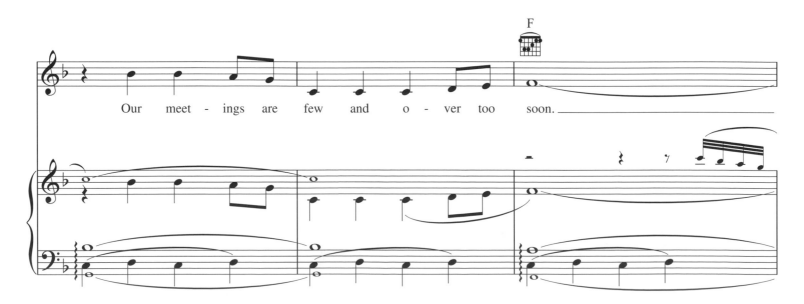

sigh    For one smil - ing day to be free    To kiss in the sun - light    And say to the sky    Be - hold and be - lieve what you see!

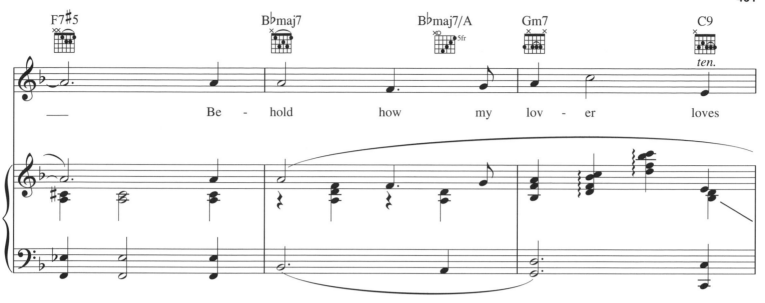

Be - hold how my lov - er loves

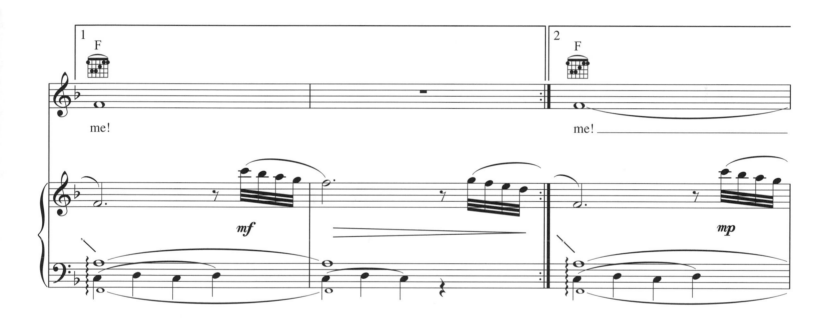

me! me!

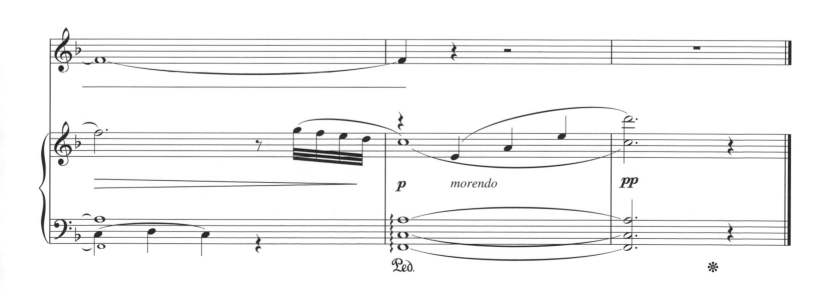

# WE'VE ONLY JUST BEGUN

Words and Music by ROGER NICHOLS
and PAUL WILLIAMS

# WHEN YOU WISH UPON A STAR

Words by NED WASHINGTON
Music by LEIGH HARLINE

# WHAT A WONDERFUL WORLD

Words and Music by GEORGE DAVID WEISS
and BOB THIELE

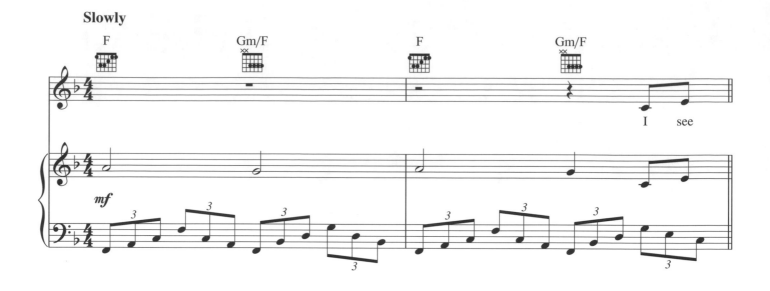

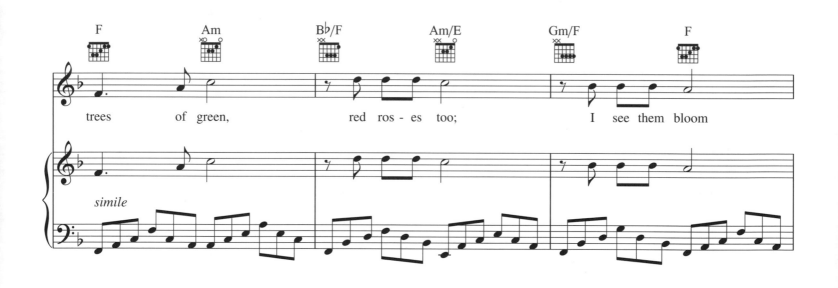

# WHAT KIND OF FOOL AM I?
from the Musical Production STOP THE WORLD—I WANT TO GET OFF

Words and Music by LESLIE BRICUSSE
and ANTHONY NEWLEY

# WHAT'LL I DO?

## from MUSIC BOX REVUE OF 1924

Words and Music by
IRVING BERLIN

**Moderate Waltz**

Gone is the ro - mance that was so di -
Do you re - mem - ber that a night so filled with

vine. _____ 'Tis bro - ken and can - not be
bliss? _____ The moon - light was soft - ly de -

mend - ed. You must go
scend - ing. Your lips and

# WHEN I FALL IN LOVE

from ONE MINUTE TO ZERO

Words by EDWARD HEYMAN
Music by VICTOR YOUNG

# WHERE DO I BEGIN
## (Love Theme)
### from the Paramount Picture LOVE STORY

Words by CARL SIGMAN
Music by FRANCIS LAI

# WHERE OR WHEN
## from BABES IN ARMS

Words by LORENZ HART
Music by RICHARD RODGERS

# WHO CAN I TURN TO
## (When Nobody Needs Me)
### from THE ROAR OF THE GREASEPAINT—THE SMELL OF THE CROWD

Words and Music by LESLIE BRICUSSE
and ANTHONY NEWLEY

# WILLOW WEEP FOR ME

Words and Music by
ANN RONELL

# YELLOW DAYS

English Lyric by ALAN BERNSTEIN
Music and Spanish Lyric by ALVARO CARRILLO

With An Easy Flow

(English) I re-
(Spanish) Se te ol-

mem-ber when the sun-light had a spe-cial kind of bright-ness, And the
vi-da que me quie-res a pe-sar de lo que di-ces, pues lle-

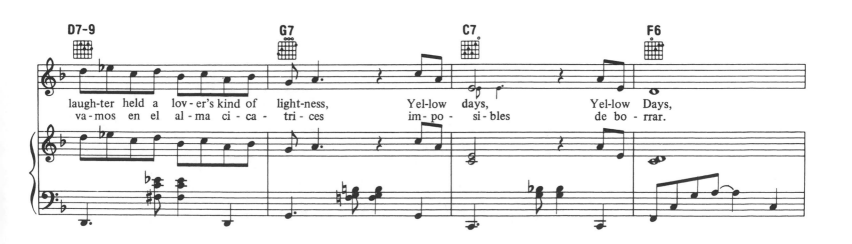

laugh-ter held a lov-er's kind of light-ness, Yel-low days, Yel-low Days,
va-mos en el al-ma ci-ca-tri-ces im-po-si-bles de bo-rrar.

# YESTERDAY

Words and Music by JOHN LENNON
and PAUL McCARTNEY

Moderately, with expression

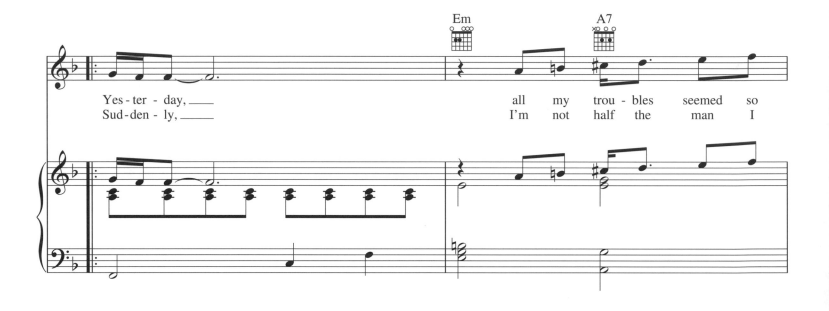

Yes - ter - day, ___ all my trou - bles seemed so
Sud - den - ly, ___ I'm not half the man I

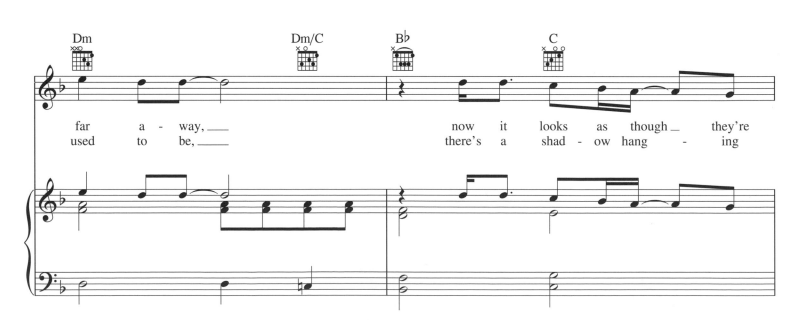

far a - way, ___ now it looks as though ___ they're
used to be, ___ there's a shad - ow hang - ing

# YOU ARE SO BEAUTIFUL

Words and Music by BILLY PRESTON
and BRUCE FISHER

# YESTERDAY ONCE MORE

Words and Music by JOHN BETTIS
and RICHARD CARPENTER

**Moderate Ballad**

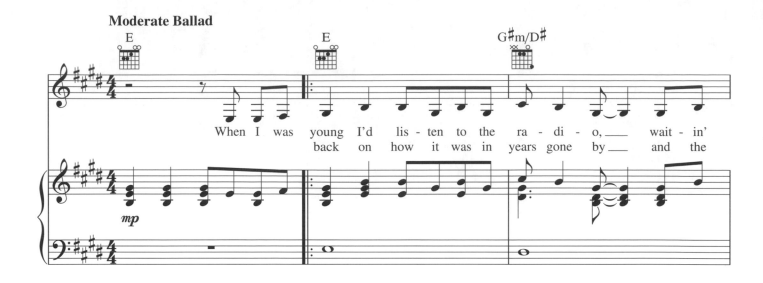

When I was young I'd lis-ten to the ra-di-o,___ wait-in'
back on how it was in years gone by ___ and the

for my fa-v'rite songs. ___ When they played, I'd sing a-long; ___
good times that I had, ___ makes to-day seem rath-er sad; ___

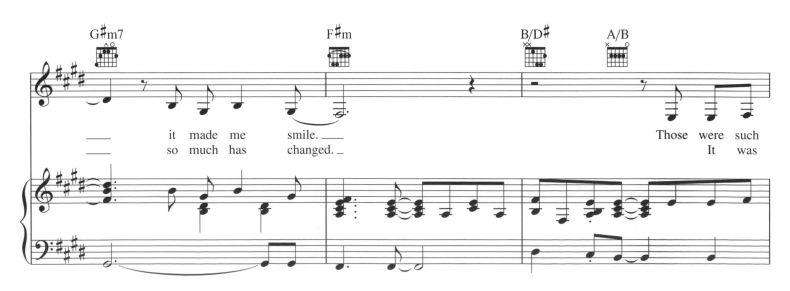

___ it made me smile. ___ Those were such
___ so much has changed. ___ It was

# YESTERDAY, WHEN I WAS YOUNG
## (Hier Encore)

English Lyric by HERBERT KRETZMER
Original French Text and Music by CHARLES AZNAVOUR

Moderately

# YOU ARE BEAUTIFUL

## from FLOWER DRUM SONG

Lyrics by OSCAR HAMMERSTEIN II
Music by RICHARD RODGERS

A - long the Hwang Ho

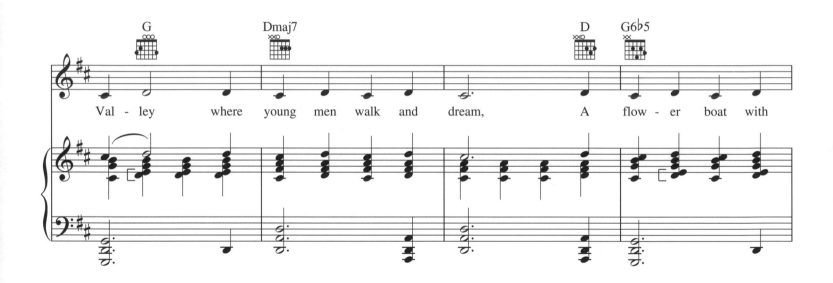

Val - ley where young men walk and dream, A flow - er boat with

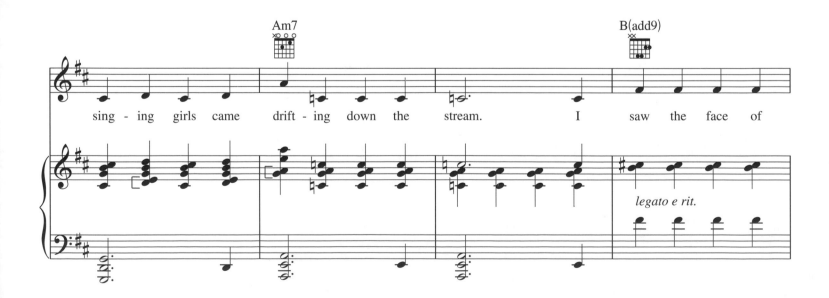

sing - ing girls came drift - ing down the stream. I saw the face of

*legato e rit.*

# YOU ARE THE SUNSHINE
# OF MY LIFE

Words and Music by
STEVIE WONDER

# YOU NEEDED ME

Words and Music by
RANDY GOODRUM

# YOU LIGHT UP MY LIFE

Words and Music by
JOSEPH BROOKS

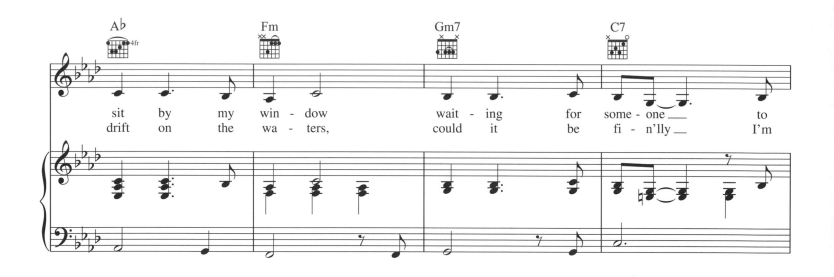

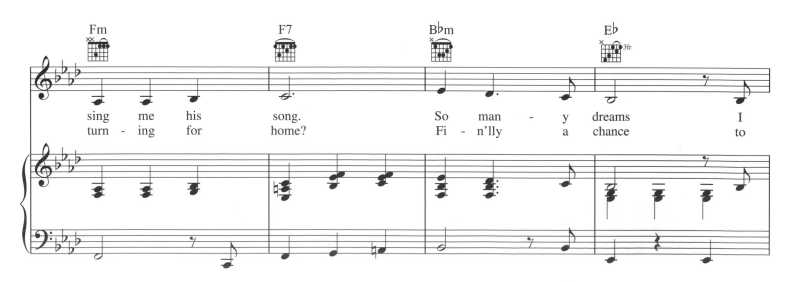

# YOUNGER THAN SPRINGTIME

## from SOUTH PACIFIC

Lyrics by OSCAR HAMMERSTEIN II
Music by RICHARD RODGERS

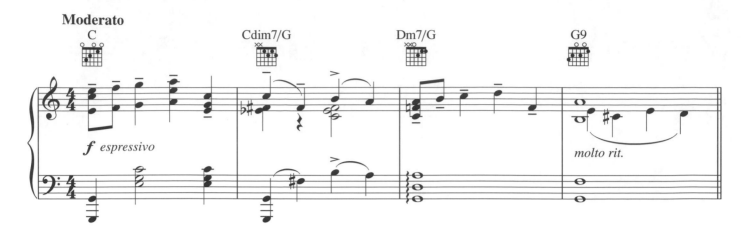

**Moderato**

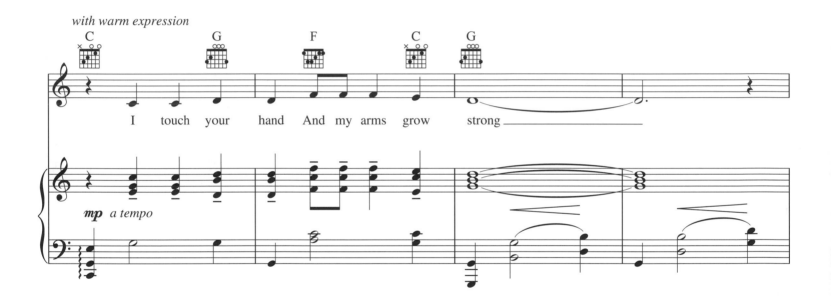

I touch your hand And my arms grow strong _____

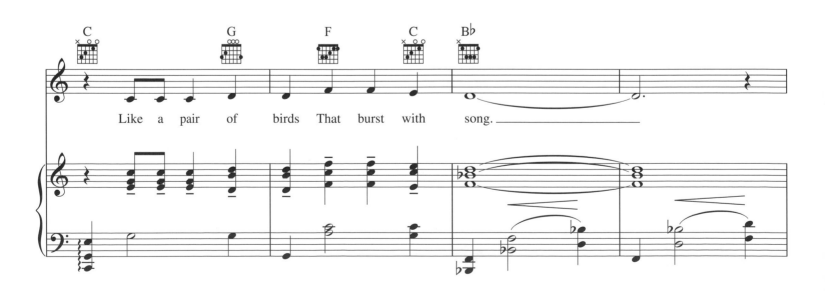

Like a pair of birds That burst with song. _____

**Refrain** (*slowly, with great warmth*)

# YOUNG AT HEART

Words by CAROLYN LEIGH
Music by JOHNNY RICHARDS

Fair-y tales __ can come true, __ it can hap-pen to you __ if you're young at heart. __ For it's hard __ you will find, __ to be nar-row of mind __ if you're young at heart. __ You can